ESSEX
RAMBLES
Ten Country Walks
around Essex

199

ESSEX RAMBLES
Ten Country Walks around Essex

Derek Keeble

———

With Historical Notes

COUNTRYSIDE BOOKS
NEWBURY, BERKSHIRE

COUNTRYSIDE BOOKS
3 Catherine Road
Newbury, Berkshire

ISBN 1 85306 006 2

Cover photograph by Andy Williams
Sketch maps by Roy Tover Graphics
Produced through MRM (Print Consultants) Ltd., Reading
Typeset by Acorn Bookwork, Salisbury
Printed in England by J.W. Arrowsmith Ltd., Bristol

Contents

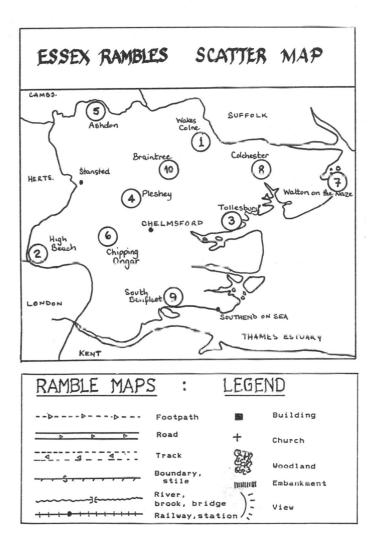

ESSEX RAMBLES   SCATTER MAP

CAMBS.

5 Ashdon

Wakes Colne

SUFFOLK

1

Braintree

10

Colchester

8

Stansted

HERTS.

4 Pleshey

Walton on the Naze

7

Tollesbury

3

CHELMSFORD

High Beach

6

2

Chipping Ongar

LONDON

South Benfleet

9

SOUTHEND ON SEA

THAMES ESTUARY

KENT

RAMBLE MAPS   :   LEGEND

`- -▷- - - -▷- - -▷- - -` Footpath	▪ Building
`═══▷═══▷═══▷═` Road	✝ Church
`- - -◁- - -◁- - -◁- - -` Track	Woodland
`┬──S──┬────┬─` Boundary, stile	ⱴⱴⱴ Embankment
`∿∿∿∿─)€─∿∿∿∿` River, brook, bridge	View
`+++++●++++++++` Railway, station	

Introduction

The walks in this book have been chosen because they offer a good variety of the county's diversity of delightful scenery. This ranges from its beautiful coastline and estuaries, each one a haven for wild-life and birds, through arable farmland and country towns to the dramatic chalk heights of north west Essex.

Each ramble has its own particular charm and point of interest. At the same time they are leisurely, enjoyable affairs which can be walked in an easy morning or afternoon.

All the walks are circular and their starting points have space for car parking. Public transport is shown where it is available. For those who like to break their walk for refreshment the names of good pubs and places serving tea along or near the route are mentioned.

The historical notes are designed to provide basic information about the places of interest along the route, and will be found at the end of each chapter.

The sketch map that accompanies each walk is designed to guide walkers to the starting point and give a simple but accurate idea of the route to be taken. For those who like the benefit of detailed maps the relevant Ordnance Survey Pathfinder sheets 1:25000 are recommended.

The walks are all along public footpaths and highways, but do bear in mind that deviation orders may be made from time to time. Please remember the Country Code and make sure gates are not left open nor any farm animals disturbed.

No special equipment is needed to enjoy the countryside on foot, but do wear a stout pair of shoes and remember that at least one muddy patch is likely even on the sunniest day.

My special thanks go to the late Jim King of Barking. His lifelong effort epitomises all the voluntary co-operation needed to make these walks possible. His encouragement will not be forgotten. Others to thank include landworkers who are good caretakers of their fields, landlords who served me with welcome beer, conservationists who monitor and remedy the plight of our wildlife and local footpath groups who repair stiles and signs and replace bridges removed by drainage contractors. Thanks to everyone who allows the simple pleasure of walking in the countryside.

A lot of enjoyment has gone into preparing these walks. I hope you will enjoy them too.

Derek Keeble
March 1988

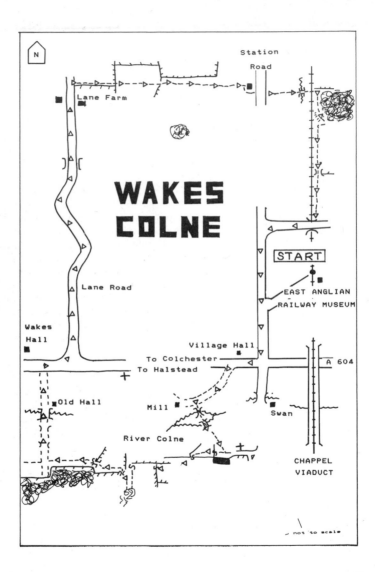

The Colne Valley at Chappel

Introduction: A visit to the beautiful Colne River Valley anywhere along its Essex length will be rewarding. This fine valley is particularly enhanced at the point where it is straddled by a viaduct at Chappel. The span of high arches defines the dimensions of the valley. The brickwork backdrop can reflect the afternoon sunlight onto the two villages of Chappel and Wakes Colne, to highlight their charming twin settlements astride the river's bright surface. A rail service is still carried aloft on the branch line from Marks Tey to Sudbury in Suffolk.

Starting from the local station, this walk explores part of the wooded southern flank of the nearby Colne valley, and returns to the East Anglian Railway Museum. Here on a site shared with the station, there is much of interest to see from the steam age of the railways.

Distance: The walking distance of 6 kilometres gives a strolling time of about 1½ hours. Ordnance Survey sheet TL 82 covers the route at the pathfinders' scale of 1:25 000. The ramble is described clockwise from the East Anglian Railway Museum map referenced TL 897289.

Refreshments: The Swan Inn at Chappel has a riverside park and garden, and is well-known for its restaurant. The East Anglian Railway Museum has a buffet car serving light meals and refreshments.

How to get there: By road; look for the landmark of the Chappel viaduct which towers above the A604 road between Halstead and Colchester. The Museum and the Station are on Station

Road signposted northwards from the crossroads beneath the
Chappel viaduct. Parking is at the Station Approach. By bus; the
stop for services 88 and 188 is at the crossroads beneath the
viaduct. By rail; make for Chappel & Wakes Colne Station on the
Sudbury to Colchester Paytrain.

The Walk: A downhill beginning helps to ease leg and other
muscles into action. Turn left in front of the dwelling 'Kismet'
when leaving the Station Approach and joining Station Road.
Continue downhill to the crossroads by Eaton's Foodstore.
Opposite is the villages' pretty double signboard, and behind it,
the river garden of the Swan in Chappel.

Stay in Wakes Colne by using the A604 road right as far
as Mill Lane just beyond the Village Hall. Fork left onto the lane
before the blacksmithy is reached. Along the lane, when the
millhouse is ahead of you, look for the footbridge on the left.
This bridge crosses the leat waters from the mill, and the
continuing path leads to a larger bridge.

Cross the second bridge and follow the path to the farmyard
by the 14th Century church at Chappel. Cross to the track in
front of the barn ahead, and turn right, to go away from the
church and the viaduct. At the north west corner of the barn, a
gate and stile give access to the waterside paddock. The upper
hedge, on the left hand side steers the path across the paddock
into a narrowing of the grazing tract caused by a meander in the
river. Use the corner stile to get into the upper field and turn
right to maintain your former direction. The path becomes part
of a tractor track until the track enters the next field, whereupon
the path pursues its own line on the upper left side of the bank.

The journey through this second field since the barn, is now
completed with a hedge on the right hand side as far as the
corner stile. A boundary on the right hand side again acts as a
handrail in the third field as far, again, as its corner stile.

The stile leads on to a green lane ascending the valley to Oak
Lane, but penetration is limited to a few metres as used by
tractors. Above their marks, the lane is choked by the over-
growth of its two hedges. Where the tractor marks turn right to a
field entrance there is also a plank bridge crossing the perimeter
ditch to a stile in the fence of the watermeadow. Take this route
and then follow the left hand boundary of this rough pasture,

rounding the corner of a woodland to find the next footbridge and stile in the grazing land.

Nearby, stands of trees are outliers from the larger Chalkney Woods which adorn this part of the valley. Continue with the boundary on the left hand side until it turns away uphill. Fen Hill Lane descends the valley here, parallel to the previous green lane, but easier to use, since this one carries a right of way.

Turn to the right and go down Fen Hill Lane to re-cross the river Colne. Pass the vestigal trees of the Lane's former hedge-line to find the first bridge over a cut-off river course. Tractors etch the route over the grass to succeeding bridges until the main river Colne bridge is reached. Pass by Old Hall Farm on the northern side to climb by the farm drive to the A604 opposite Wakes Hall. The mature trees alongside the road frame the view of Wakes Colne's exquisite church to the right. The pavement is on the Wakes Hall side of the road and the walk goes eastwards, away from the craftshop and garden centre there. Turn left off the A604 where a chestnut tree covers a triangular junction with a country lane.

Follow Lane Road to pass Cymbeline and Crows Hall, and to go over the old railway bridge and to find Lane Farm. When you get beyond the farm buildings, use the field edge path right to the chestnut tree in the corner by the pole. A path, re-instated after cultivation, crosses to the oak tree in the opposite hedge. Here the path resumes its field edge character and re-aligns with the overhead wires. For its final section, the path reverts to its reinstated status before crossing behind the single dwelling, and then beside it, to get to the road. Directly opposite, another waymark indicates the continuation path. This too has its route reinstated after cultivation, as do many paths in the fertile arable acres of Essex. The path leads to a footbridge by the railway kissing-gate stiles. Cross the railway line at the level crossing to enter the woods and turn right underneath the canopy made by sycamore trees. Keep the railway fence in view, even where a bank diverges slightly from it. The path drops off the bank and leaves the woodland corner to become a headland walk beside the railway hedge along two fields.

A stile in a gap of the blackthorn hedge leads you to Spring Garden Road beside the railway bridge. From the top of the bridge there is a good overview of the East Anglian Railway

Museum marshalling yard alongside Chappel and Wakes Colne Station platform. Go right by Orchard Cottage and left at the junction of roads. Go down Station Road again to find the Museum's signal at the beginning of the same station approach from which you began the walk.

Historical Notes

Chappel Viaduct dates from 1847 when 7 million bricks were made to assemble its 30 arches in fine Victorian form 324 metres above the River Colne.

Chalkney Woods contain one of the best stands of small-leaf lime trees in the county. It is a public amenity woodland where the coppice cycle is worked as a conservation exercise. The spread of wild flowers is best seen by the upper section of hardwoods.

Wakes Hall, with its craft shops and garden centre, is maintained by the Stars Organisation for Spastics. The building dates from the early 1840s.

Bridge over Lane Road crosses the former Colne Valley single track line from Chappel & Wakes Colne junction to Haverhill, where it re-united with the Stour Valley line. It was probably one of the early Beeching closures. The Colne Valley Steam Preservation Centre at Castle Hedingham is on this old line too.

East Anglia Railway Museum Chappel & Wakes Colne station, once a busy junction serving lines northwards to Haverhill or Bury St Edmunds, is today the home of East Anglia Railway Museum operated by the Stour Valley Preservation Society.

During summer months, industrial locomotives *Jubilee* or *Penn Green* haul ex-BR Mk 1 coaches along a ½ mile stretch of track in the station's old goods yard. In addition work continues to restore further locomotives plus a collection of pre-1900 six and four-wheel passenger stock to form a vintage train. The Society has hopes for the future. Eyes are looking towards

Bures, some 4 miles to the north, either sharing the existing single-track with BR or even one day building their own alongside.

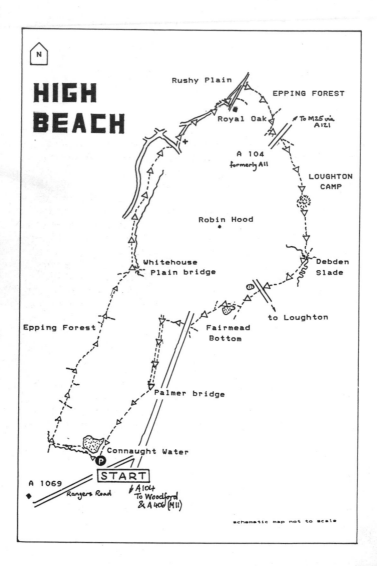

N

HIGH BEACH

Rushy Plain

EPPING FOREST

Royal Oak

To M25 via A121

A 104
formerly A11

LOUGHTON CAMP

Robin Hood

Whitehouse Plain bridge

Debden Slade

Epping Forest

Fairmead Bottom

to Loughton

Palmer bridge

Connaught Water

P

START

A 1069

Rangers Road

A104
To Woodford & A406 (M11)

schematic map not to scale

16

Epping Forest

Introduction: Epping Forest has meant so much to people of this and other centuries, and it is likely to do so in the future. Queen Victoria dedicated the forest around High Beach for the enjoyment of the people for ever. And there it remains, a precarious buffer between the metropolitan capital city and the urban fringes of Essex. It is cut by the administrative boundary between Essex and Greater London Boroughs, is tunnelled by the capital's orbital motorway, and still its canopy of broadleaves covers a plethora of interests and pleasures. No other place in Essex can provide a similar wilderness with such a wide range of woodland walking. It is perhaps ironic that many Essex and Hertfordshire people, seeking a day's walk in the countryside, turn their steering wheels towards London rather than away from it in order to enjoy Epping Forest.

This predominantly forest walk is varied by visits to a small settlement, a couple of pubs, some open spaces and an iron age hill fort.

Distance: The distance of 8 kilometres takes about 2 hours to stroll. Ordnance Survey sheet TQ 49 covers the route at the pathfinders' scale of 1:25 000. The walk is described clockwise starting from the carpark by Connaught Water, map referenced TQ 405951.

Refreshments: The Royal Forest, Rangers Road, London E4; The Butlers Retreat, Rangers Road, London E4; The Royal Oak, High Beach; The Robin Hood on the A104 Roundabout in Epping Forest, and Mobile kiosk at popular times on Rushy Plain by Claygate Hill.

How to get there: By road; from Junction 26 of the M25, use the A121 towards Loughton. Pass the Volunteer and The Woodbine

17

to find the roundabout junction by the City Limits. Exit by the A104 Woodford Road. Continue on the A104 beyond the Robin Hood and pass The Warren, The Corporation of London's Epping Forest Headquarters. By The Warren the A1069 Rangers Road to Chingford forks right. Turn here to find Connaught Water car park 350 metres along the right hand side. It is a Pay and Display Car Park. By train; Loughton Station, on the Central Line, is 1.6 kilometres away from the walk route. By bus; numerous bus services go to Loughton and to Chingford. Queen Elizabeth Hunting Lodge, some 500 metres along Rangers Road from the car park, is served by buses.

The Walk: The lake at the car park is a natural attraction. Walk around it clockwise and cross the concrete bridge over the outfall stream. A myriad of minor paths slope in or around the southern edge of the taller vegetation there. Use any one of these to head westwards for 200 metres. It takes 3 minutes to walk but the feature sought cannot be missed. It is a 3 metre wide ride for horses. Dressed with hoggin, the ride has a warm contrasting colour to the surrounding vegetation. Rides such as this one are good navigational aids in the forest.

Turn right onto the path and head away from the A1069 road. Now very close to the boundary of Essex with Greater London at Magpie Hill the path can easily be followed if not actually walked upon. Horse hooves can cause very muddy conditions in places: too uncomfortable to walk through. Minor paths braid either side to offer by-passes. Walking beneath the giant trees is a pleasant experience denied us far too frequently. Another major track joins from the south-west and very soon a crosstrack junction is reached. Continue ahead, with ground rising gently by Cuckoo Pits to a staggered junction, right first. Ignore both turnings and the next crossing of major tracks where triangular junctions have been formed.

Some 25 minutes after joining the track, it leaves the shelter of the trees for a vast grassy plain. The first section, called Almhouse Plain, steers the track towards a bridging point where Whitehouse Plain is met. Don't cross the bridge but instead go left of it. The gradient increases and there is no more track to steer by. Instead there is Church Road, with vehicles, over to the left, and the little stream on the right wending its way back to the bridge on the Plain.

Continue northwards, using the road and stream as left and right handrails respectively. As the climb progresses, a minor path from the vicarage converges from the left. Follow this north-eastwards to cross the road by High Beach church. This high standing church is a popular landmark to find in the forest. Continue northwards along the road west of the church to pass the Youth Hostel's turning and emerge on the sandy edge of Rushy Plain by the Kings Oak Hotel.

Good views to the Lea Valley are to the left, and over the other shoulder is the hotel and the entrance for the Conservation Centre. North of these two, by a forked road junction, another of the hoggin surfaced rides begins. It starts off south-eastwards and then sweeps around behind the Centre and the hotel to join with another track coming in from the left.

Soon the track begins to dip into a small but steep-sided valley. Turn left onto the path going towards the A104 road. Parallel on the right hand side is the little valley, rapidly getting deeper. Young birch trees survive here. Cross the main road with caution and find the continuation track opposite. Take the right fork to remain parallel with the valley.

The path stays on its higher route to enter the folds of land marking the remains of the iron age hill fort known now as Loughton Camp.

Unseen in Woodbury Hollow, to the south of the camp, is a right angle formed where the stream is bridged by another of those hoggin tracks. Leave the camp by any of the minor paths heading south to south eastwards and find the bridge.

Cross the bridge and head southwards up a steep gradient. Below to the left, roots are washed by the contorted meanders of Debden Slade. At the top of the gradient another road has to be crossed. The track continues by a pond and within 200 metres passes another larger pond. Contented-looking anglers frequent the edges of both.

Turn right off the track before passing this second pond. A path follows the edge of the water under the trees to a clearing on the western side. The line of the path can still be seen in the grass, over to an anti-vehicle log marking its continuation under the further canopy of trees.

All the paths so far have been pleasant, and this one over Fairmead Bottom, so close to The Warren, is extremely enjoyable to walk. Re-cross the A104 road and turn left to be parallel with it down to Palmer Bridge. This bridge is over a now disused side road.

Cross the bridge and ignore the cinder track in preference for the south westward headed path. This leads very gently downhill over two wooden bridges to the northern edge of Connaught Water. Walk around either edge of the lake, and you will find the car park where the walk began.

Historical Notes

Essex Boundary: The outflow from Connaught Water forms the stream crossed by the A1069 road. This has formed the Essex boundary since the formation of the Greater London Council in the early 1960s. Most, but not all of the forest is in Essex. The neighbouring London Boroughs were formerly ratepayers to Essex County.

Queen Elizabeth's Hunting Lodge in Rangers Road is now the Corporation of London's Epping Forest Museum, administered by the Conservators of Epping Forest. It is open to the public from 2pm to dusk or 6pm daily except Mondays and Tuesdays.

Epping Forest: The forest covers an area of about 6,000 acres. Before the Civil War it covered about 60,000 acres. Felling trees for the navy and later the Enclosure Movement reduced it to its present size. In the late 19th century the forest was purchased for £250,000 and Queen Victoria visited High Beach on 6th May 1882 to dedicate the forest for the enjoyment of the public in perpetuity.

Loughton Camp is an early Iron Age encampment, roughly oval in shape and covering about 6½ acres.

Tollesbury and the Blackwater Estuary

Introduction: Essex has many waterside settlements where boating and fishing activities are so interlocked as to totally enchant land-lubbers. Tollesbury is one such place. It is an old fishing community which surprises many. Northwards across the saltmarshes of Old Hall Creek it is bounded by the energetically managed Royal Society for the Protection of Birds Nature Reserve. Southwards, over the seawall, is the wide Blackwater Estuary. This grand and beautiful estuary is one of the largest on the eastern coast between the Humber and the Thames.

Snugly centred is the flourishing and bustling community that is distinctly Tollesbury.

Distance: A walking distance of 10 kilometres to give a strolling time of 2½ hours. Ordnance Survey sheet TL 91 at the pathfinders' scale of 1:25 000, covers most of the route, with an easily navigated 350 metres on sheet TL 90.

Starting from the village car park on Woodrolfe Road, map referenced TL 963106, the route is described anti-clockwise.

Refreshments: *The Hope Inn*, High Street, Tollesbury and *The Kings Head* on the corner of Church Square both serve food.

How to get there: By road; Tollesbury is a coastal village on the B1023, which is approached from the A12 trunk road via Kelvedon and Tiptree. Leave the A12 and enter Kelvedon to find the B1023 road junction at the top of Feering Hill. Cross over the B1022 road in Tiptree and join the B1026 road right in Tolleshunt D'Arcy for 350 metres before turning left at the Red Lion for a continuation of the B1023 road into Tollesbury.

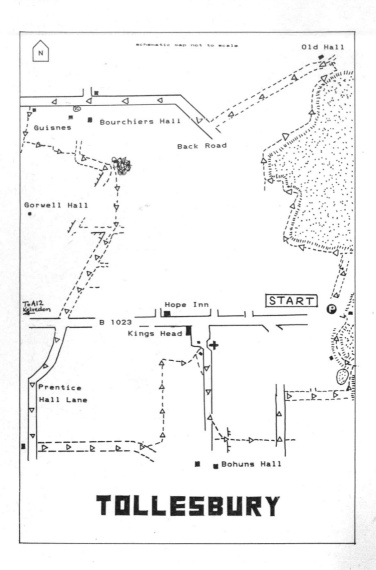

Continue beyond Church Square along East Street to the forked junction, Mell Road with Woodrolfe Road. Go left to find the car park almost at sea level just before Woodrolfe marina. The Woodrolfe car park also houses the Baden-Powell Centre.

By rail; nearest station is Kelvedon. Transfer to bus. By bus; Osborne's buses serve Witham, Maldon and Colchester from their Tollesbury garage off East Street.

The Walk: A concrete track heads northwards from the Baden-Powell Centre. Use this right of way to join the seawall by the treatment plant. Go left to follow the seawall as it weaves around Old Hall Creek to Old Hall Farm. The building acting as a landmark is the Ship Ahoy, alas no longer a pub. Its array of dormer windows signal the point to leave the seawall. Go left again, this time on Old Hall Lane which soon becomes a metalled track.

The saltmarshes and mudflats of the Blackwater, as exampled here at Old Hall, are internationally known as a winter migrating refuge for huge numbers of waders and wildfowl. Brent geese flock here to bring their own primeval music to the marshes in wintertime.

Turn right onto Back Road and walk towards Tolleshunt D'Arcy. Pass Bourchiers Hall, Colchester Road turning and Guisnes Court to find Guisnes Gate Cottage opposite the trees of The Grove.

Take the field edge path waymarked beside the cottage. Continue on the path beyond the end of the garden to the first field boundary left. Here two bridges under the trees offer a crossing of the ditch to the field edge path going off left. Pens for fowls are housed on the left hand grasses, whilst arable crops close in on the right hand side.

The right of way diverges slightly right of this crop-change, but the worn path follows the obvious line to the hedge corner behind Bourchiers Hall. Go right here to the nearby wire-carrying pole, then turn left to follow a change-crop alignment which marks with the right of way. This line becomes a headland track and heads towards the stand of broadleaved trees one more field away at The Rookery.

By the corner of the trees, the headland deflects right, and follows the field edge around to the tree to be seen straight ahead. The right of way is reinstated on the direct line. Re-united with the headland, follow it southwards to the B1023 crossroads. Cross straight over here and continue down the lane by Garlands Farm which is Prentice Hall Lane. Continue southwards along it as far as the next farmhouses.

Turn left onto a wide headland and head eastwards to Bohuns Hall. The soils of the fields down by the Blackwater appear to be russet red. The redness is said to have occurred with the ploughing in of red hills.

The headland deflects right for the farmyard, but the path continues straight ahead for the recreation ground lined with poplar trees. Follow the western boundary of the area to the tennis courts and then veer right to the exit by the pavilion. The cage and St Mary's Church are nearby. Return southwards by the walled pond on Church Road, and enter the paddock via a stile on the left hand side. Continue across the paddock on a worn path, to the stile shared by another path. The excellent mid-field path, offering good views, continues eastwards to Mell Road.

Turn left to enter the housing zone and turn right by the telephone booth to enter Woodrolfe Lane. This unmade road has ribbon development down to Woodrolfe Farm. Leave the farmyard on the left and continue downhill, between hedges high enough to form a tunnel, to the seawall. Swing left as the path bisects the cluster of lagoons to climb to the seawall by Tollesbury Marina. Turn left to pass over Tollesbury Cruising Centre's paths to the slipways, and to continue by the open swimming pool to the sail lofts which are the focal interest of the industrial, fishing and recreational activities at Woodrolfe Creek. The car park is a few metres along the road left towards the village square.

Historical Notes

Bird Sanctuary: Old Hall Marshes Farm (just east of Old Hall farm) is managed by the Royal Society for the Protection of Birds from its headquarters in Sandy. The grazing system used on the marshes produces an optimum habitat for marshland breeding birds.

Tolleshunt D'Arcy saw the development of the D'arcy Spice Apple in 1785. This apple was grown commercially later in mid-Essex orchards.

Red Hills: Samples of these phenomena were closely examined earlier this century. Current thinking is that the redness is residual from Roman firings to evaporate brine, and so procure the salt. Saltmaking by evaporation still continues further up the Blackwater today at Maldon.

The Cage: A lock-up dating from 1700 is preserved in Church Square by dwelling number 7.

St Mary's Church: St Mary's strong square tower which was heightened about 1600, is a landmark for mariners negotiating Shinglehead and Woodrolfe Creek. A stained glass window by Kempe in 1902 depicts Tollesbury's marine and fishing traditions. Inside, the font attracts humourous interest, although modern soccer followers may not be amused! Its inscription reads: 'Good people all I pray take care, That in ye church you do not sware. As this man did'.

Tollesbury: The Sail lofts of 1902 Essex weatherboard are at the heart of romantic Tollesbury. Tollesbury is a noted fishing centre with a cherished reputation for fine sprats and dabs as well as oysters and other shellfish. As a centre for the skills of sailing it had representatives on Sir Thomas Lipton's and Tommy Sopwith's crafts challenging for the pre-war Americas Cup.

Evidence of former railway tracks crossing the ramble's route may be found in Old Hall Lane and Woodrolfe Lane. The former level crossing closed as part of the Beeching package which ended the Kelvedon to Tollesbury 'Crab and Winkle' Line. The latter crossing closed earlier when the extension from Tollesbury Station to Tollesbury Pier lost its commercial and military viability. Since the great flood of 1953, the pier remnants by Mell Creek have been almost unrecognisable.

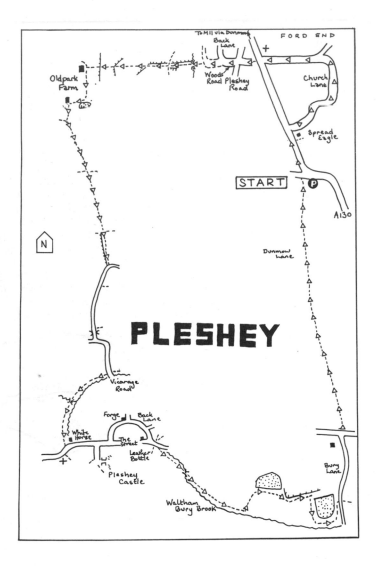

FORD END

To Mil via Dunmow
Back Lane

Oldpark Farm

Woods Road   Pleshey Road

Church Lane

Spread Eagle

START   P

A130

N

Dunmow Lane

PLESHEY

Vicarage Road

Forge   Back Lane

White Horse

The Street

Leather Bottle

Pleshey Castle

Bury Lane

Waltham Bury Brook

Pleshey Castle

Introduction: Pleshey, Ford End and Great Waltham are all part of the Chelmsford Borough Council's district. There has been a rapid rise of interest in walking within the district in recent years. Attractive waymarking with yellow butterfly emblems, known affectionately as the Chelmsford Footillery, is both the result and the enhancement of the interest. The work to refurbish rural field paths is complemented in the city of Chelmsford, where a network of traffic-free cycle lanes and pedestrian ways is in vigorous use.

Pleshey Castle, with its village still enveloped within its moat, is the main attraction of this ramble. It is situated by the watershed between the rivers Can and Chelmer on the clay lands of arable Essex. Dunmow Lane, used on the return from Pleshey to Ford End, is a green lane to cherish. It is a remnant of the many ancient lanes once found in Essex, and now very important for conservationists.

Distance: The walking distance of 11 kilometres takes about 3 hours to stroll. Ordnance Survey sheet TL 61 covers the route at the pathfinders' scale of 1:25 000. The ramble is described anti-clockwise, starting from the Stumps Cross lay-by on the A130 road south of Ford End church and map referenced TL 682164.

Refreshments: The Spread Eagle at Ford End is alongside the A130 just north of the starting place at Stumps Cross.

The Leather Bottle in Pleshey is found by turning right of Back Lane just after passing Woolmers Mead. The White Horse is situated in Pleshey, by the church.

How to get there: Stumps Cross is found on the Dunmow to Chelmsford section of the A130, near the junction with the B1417, some 5 miles from Great Dunmow.

The Walk: From the Stumps Cross layby, head northwards along the A130 as far as the Spread Eagle. Cross with care to enter Church Lane. This leafy lane takes a quiet excursion around to attractive housing by Ford End Church.

The views to the right are over the Chelmer valley, and the large building nestled by the river is a brewery.

Re-cross the main road by the telephone kiosk and enter the pedestrians' end of Woods Road. Continue to cross Pleshey Road by the red post box and so enter Back Lane.

As Back Lane hooks around to encircle the housing, so a track continues ahead and downhill. Use the track until it also hooks to the right. Again continue straight ahead, now on a headland descending to a bridge over a stream.

Climb up from the stream, keeping the hedge on the right hand side, until near the top the path enters a double hedged section. After this section the route continues westwards as a field edge path with the hedge again on the right hand side. At the next corner, use the bridge to get to the outside of the hedge corner, and then follow the re-instated path across to the concave far corner of the next arable field. A distant view across the Chelmer valley to the right includes the settlement of Felsted and its sugar-beet factory by its Little Dunmow outpost. Again there is a bridge in the corner. This one links to a path exposed between the crops leading to a three-barred gate. Behind the gate is Oldpark Farm with a silo prominent amidst its buildings. From the gate, cross the grazing towards the silo. Turn left by the cattle grid and overhead hopper, before the buildings, and follow the farm track around to pass between the farmhouse and the farm ponds, where a gaggle of geese may attempt an escort service.

An uphill concrete drive begins the walk to Pleshey. At the top T-junction turn left and Pleshey's fine church comes in view. The concrete bi-strip track leads easily and gradually down to an acute bend on Park Road. Go right, to cross Post Bridge at the end of Park Road. Go left, to climb Vicarage Road towards Pleshey. As the housing zone is reached, so the outer earthworks come in view. Go right on the path which follows the outer rim of the ramparts, crossing one bridge, before finding Holy Trinity Church and the White Horse on either side of The Street.

By St Michael's Cottage on The Street is the junction with Pump Lane, labelled 'Private, Lodge Farm'. But it is along this lane, beyond Castle Cottage and before the private part, that admirable views of Pleshey's castle remains may be made.

Further along The Street, turn left by the Post Office, and find the Forge around by the junction of Back Lane with Vicarage Road. There is a social cheerfulness around the smithy. Back Lane rejoins The Street by the old Mission Hall. Go left and pass Mount House to find several waymarks. Select the path diverging right from the road and forming a gap between Walthambury brook and the chainlink fence of a sewerage treatment plant. Soon after leaving the fence corner, the brook passes beneath it, so that the field edge path follows the left hand bank of the ever-deepening water course. A footbridge is passed near a confluence of streams, and later a cartbridge gives vehicular access to a reservoir to the left. Use the track to get to the reservoir and turn right by the dam, to find the waymarked path continuing on a contour parallel to the brook. Around the curve before Bury Farm, a second reservoir is encountered. Waymarks again direct a diversion around the southern side of the water.

Turn left on Bury Lane and climb away from the ford to the T-junction of roads. Opposite a bridleway is waymarked. This is Dunmow Lane, a double hedged, soft surfaced highway leading gently uphill northwards back to Stumps Cross at Ford End.

Historical Notes

Pleshey Castle: This motte and bailey dates from the 12th century and it has a well-recorded history. Names such as De Mandeville, Fitzpiers, De Bohun, Woodstock and Mowbray are among the earldoms and dukedoms possessing Pleshey over the years. The outer bailey encloses the whole village.

Ridleys brewery at Ford End is one of several East Anglian breweries known for its strong beer. Most imbibers of real ale are aware of its existence.

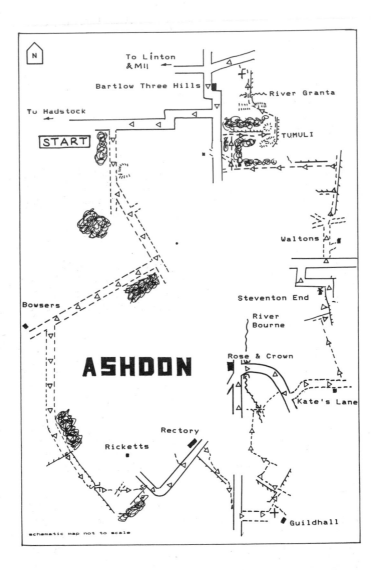

Ashdon and the Bartlow Hills

Introduction: Bartlow Hills are in Ashdon. So close are they to the parish boundary, that soil could easily creep off the tumuli into Cambridgeshire's Bartlow. This ramble is contained within the parish of Ashdon: an Essex parish of several Ends located in the northernmost tip of the county.

The area contrasts with most of remaining Essex. The soils are whiter being part of the East Anglian Heights, an extension of Chiltern chalk. The drainage is more incised; as greater height of land gives more impetus to the running waters. The direction of this run-off is northwards via the river Cam towards the Wash. Whereas all other Essex catchments flow ultimately eastwards to the North Sea.

Distance: The walking distance of 12 kilometres takes about 3 hours to stroll. Ordnance Survey sheet TL 54 covers the route at the pathfinders' scale of 1:25 000. The ramble is described anti-clockwise from Hadstock Road, by the site of the former railway junction, map referenced TL 580450.

Refreshments: The *Rose & Crown* overlooks the major road junction in Ashdon's centre, *The Bricklayers Arms* at Rogers End, downstream from the *Rose & Crown*, *The Bonnet* up at Steventon End by the windmill, and *The Three Hills* in Bartlow by the confluence of the rivers Bourne and Granta.

How to get there: By road; from the M11 junction 10, use the A505 eastwards to merge with the A11. Cross the river Granta and turn right at the roundabout on to the A604 road for Harwich. Cross the B1052 at Linton and take the next right turn off the A604. This leads to Bartlow. Turn right at the village crossroads, and right again by the saddlery. Go through the old railway bridge buttresses and park unobstructively on the wide shoulder of Hadstock Road.

The Walk: Head uphill and southwards on a stony track from the Hadstock-Bartlow Road. Select the track beginning about 100 metres west of the old railway bridge. It rises between a woodland belt on the right hand side and an old sand pit on the left. Within five minutes the track forks. Use the less steep left hand one which carries the right of way. Three more junctions are encountered before the bridge over the old Saffron Walden track is reached. The second of these is to the right opposite a lonely cottage by an old clay pit, old railway and old pump. Use this headland to resume the uphill haul. This time the trees are on the left hand side. The track crests a hill and begins to dip towards Bowsers Farm. Before it is reached, a concrete drive emanating from the farm offers a turn to the left. The right of way is not quite true to the first 100 metres of concrete, but the track is a used path. Follow its pleasant course down to its last gate beside a brook and a woodland.

Thoughtfully, the electric fencing cable is carried high over the gate to allow walkers to enter the grazing. Close the gate.

Continue beside the brook until a stile in the left hand fence indicates steps down to a footbridge hidden in the blackthorn hedge. A second stile gives access to the next grazing plot. Ricketts farmhouse, sited on the side of a knoll comes into view. The gate of the grazing is on the track leading down from the farm, but the walkers' exit is in the corner lower down from the gate.

Steps cut in the earthen bank allow the climb up through the blackthorn tunnel to emerge beside a pole at the former railway level. Turn right onto the track and follow it up to the large rectory on the left hand side at the top of the hill. Turn opposite its redbrick frontage, before the Kham Tibet house is reached, to use the track which transfers to the right hand side of the field. It leads to the road before Ashdon Hall. Go right again to find the old British National school, now making a fine centre for antiques. Cross carefully to approach the church.

On the south side of the church is a fine old guildhall. From these adjacent buildings use the eastern path to the stile at the lower end of the paddock. Turn left onto the headland against the hedge and look for the narrow path descending the field by the midfield hawthorn tree. Use this and bear left at the bottom to follow a similar path by an ash tree. Go right along the gardens' rear greensward as far as the footbridge behind the Labour Hall.

Cross the footbridge and use the left hand of the paths available. This leads across to the Baptist Church carpark in Radwinter Road by the policehouse. Opposite is Kate's Lane junction. If it is opening time, a visit to the *Rose & Crown* is rewarding. Join the road at the front of the Labour Hall and turn right. The pub is along the leafy road, at the very hub of the village. From its front door look across the river to the Conservative Hall and up Radwinter Road. That is the way to resume the Ramble.

Enter Kate's Lane by 'Chestnuts' and climb the slope of the lane until just beyond the house on the right hand standing in its garden orchard. Here a waymark points left up a clear midfield path towards the windmill.

Follow this path and veer right with the top hedge to find the gap in the hedge junction. Dip left through here and follow the hedgeline to the whitewashed cottages by the picturesque windmill. The lane bends beyond the windmill to merge with the road to Steventon End, not too far below The Bonnet.

The ensuing sequence of paths is never far from the county border with Cambridgeshire. Turn right towards Steventon End and walk by the wall on the road without a footway, as far as Ridgewells Farm on the right. Opposite is the grand entrance of Waltons. Enter here and follow the stonedash drive to the first junction. Fork left onto a tarmac drive which assumes a gravelled surface between the paddocks. The treelined drive ends at a fiveway junction. Do not take the acute left turn, nor the right hand track bounded by a brick wall. Select the right hand fork of the two remaining forward tracks, the grassier headland with a right hand hedge.

The headland loses its hedge as it swells to make a fine gallop dipping and climbing to another hedgeline. Stay with this hedgeline even when the track turns sharply left to descend the Bourne valley. Follow the upper field edge path to the next corner which is also a track junction. Fork left to use the earthen track following first the hedge and then a coniferous tree-belt down to the Bartlow Road.

The tree-belt bends right to fringe the road. Between the tree trunks runs the path. A drive from the farmbuildings crosses the road to Hill Farm. Some steps off this drive give access to this path.

Head north parallel to the road. The path steps down and up over a farmtrack, and immediately steps down again to a cross path. To the right is the site of Bartlow Hills. The three hills are enclosed, but another opening in the fence allows a second path to leave. This exit path from the northernmost hill crosses the Cambridgeshire border and the deep and empty old railway track via a high bridge.

Follow the severe and solid fencing and cross a young Granta stream under towering beech trees to find the road once through Bartlow's churchyard.

Turn left to the Bartlow village crossroads, turn left again to find the Three Hills Inn. Recross the river and turn right by the recreation ground opposite Bartlow estate entrance. Three minutes walking on the road towards Hadstock will bring you back to your parked vehicle.

Historical Notes

Railway Lines: Two former railway lines met at Bartlow junction en route for Cambridge. The one featured on this ramble looped off the existing London–Cambridge line at Audley End station in Wendens Ambo. It served Saffron Walden. The other line close to the tumuli linked to Haverhill and the Stour Valley line and its off-shoot, the Colne Valley Line.

Roman Villa: The foundations of this villa on Great Copt Hill were discovered in the 19th century. When excavated, it was found to have 7 rooms, half of them heated by a hypercaust system. A row of conifers alongside the track now mark its site.

All Saints Church: The church is mainly of the 14th century but much restored in Victorian times. It contains an interesting large tomb chest with three shields on intricate panels of the early 16th century.

Waltons: The house was begun in the Elizabethan period and has been adapted and extended in later centuries. The fine Georgian front was added in 1730.

Windmill: The post windmill at Steventon End has been restored to continue its service as a landmark, if not to grind corn anymore.

Tumuli: Bartlow Hills. Three conical burial mounds remain from the original nine. The others were sacrificed for land gain during recent centuries. The largest is 13 metres high and 43 metres in diameter.

The later ones to be erased were excavated archaeologically beforehand. Some of the artifacts found there are now in Saffron Walden Museum. The finds suggest that the site was in use as a cemetery in the 2nd century AD. Many of the finds were taken to Easton Lodge, as the property of the owner. A fire at Easton in 1847 destroyed many of the grave goods.

Nature Reserve: Shadwell Wood is a nature reserve managed by the Essex Naturalists' Trust.

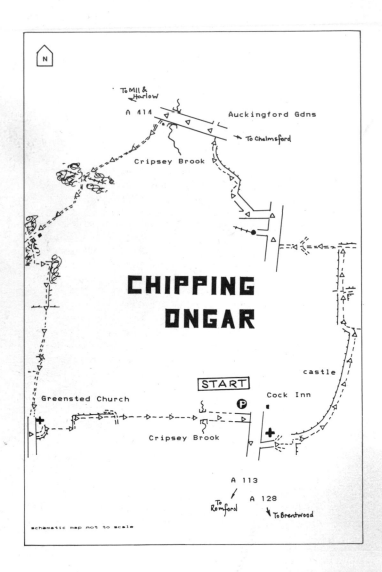

CHIPPING ONGAR

schematic map not to scale

The Log Church at Greensted

Introduction: A regular livestock market would seem strangely out of place in Chipping Ongar today. Nevertheless there has been a return to more blissful days since the completion of the London orbital motorway. The noise and fumes of Dartford Tunnel traffic has now ceased to cut the town in half.

The town enjoys its connections with London, but retains a separate identity. Its castle overlooks the confluence of Cripsey Brook with the Roding river. It is an enjoyable place to visit and its many paths are kept in good order. This ramble features a pilgrimage to the oldest 'log church' in the world at Greensted Green.

Distance: The walking distance of 6 kilometres takes about 1½ hours to stroll. Ordnance Survey sheet TL 50 covers the route at the pathfinders' scale of 1:25 000. The ramble is described anti-clockwise starting from Budworth Hall free car park in the heart of Chipping Ongar, map referenced TL 552032.

Refreshments: The Coffee Pot is adjacent to Budworth Hall clock tower, The Cock Inn adjacent to the overflow car park on the eastern side of the road, while further down the street are situated both The Kings Head and The Royal Oak. There is also a restaurant called Ruggles, about half way along the walk, on the A414.

How to get there: By road; from junction 7 on the M11 motorway select the A414 road heading eastwards for Chelmsford. Chipping Ongar is reached in 9 kilometres. At the Four Wantz Roundabout turn southwards on the A128 (A113) road. The railway station is passed on the right hand side and then the clocktower and the pedestrians' crossings come into view. Car parking is available both sides of the road. By train; Central Line terminus. Change at Epping. By bus; Routes 32, 452, 501, 391, 392, 393, 201.

The Walk: From the clocktower use the pedestrian crossing and turn downhill beyond the Kings Head to find Castle Street by Essex House and Ufford Villas. Turn in here to the street's forked eastern end. A stile by the lamp post labelled Spring Meadow is central to the fork.

The ensuing path soon begets headland status as it swings left between fences parallel to the curve of the castle moat. Beyond the moat continue northwards on a similar headland to its turn by the recreation ground. Ignore the left stile, and enter the playground by the swings and slide. A surfaced path follows the left hand hedge to the corner by the housing. Turn left to find a superior surface on the hedged path westwards to emerge between the Sports & Social Centre and the Cemetery. Descend by unmade road by 'Treetops' to emerge on the main road by the Woolcabin.

Turn uphill across the top of the Station's approach and enter the next road left, signed Bowes Drive. Midway down the Drive is the junction with Marks Avenue. Turn right here and enter the field at its other end, by house number 23. Use the right hand field edge path, clearly etched on the ground, around to its gated exit on the A414 road opposite Auckingford Gardens.

The busy A414 has to be followed downhill to the bridge. There is a pavement on the northern side of the road. The bridge over Cripsey Brook dates from 1913. As the road swings away from the bridge, so the white painted restaurant comes into view. Turn left onto a bridleway which joins the road by the Ruggles entrance.

A sign on the waymark mentions the Year of the Disabled 1981 when the bridleway assumed special marking. It is a very pleasant stony track rising away from the brook towards a wooded horizon. The railway line is bridged amid a stand of oak trees: one of those points where passengers may pinch themselves to believe they are on London's underground rail system.

The bridleway continues to the cottage's vehicle turnaround, whereupon the suitability for the disabled also terminates. A sign on a nearby tree indicates a continuation path to Toothill and to Greensted Church. For a short stretch it is a rough overgrown path until it enters a small stand of trees. Under the canopy of branches the path splits. Take the left-turn path which begins with a step over a small ditch and then it leads for a short stretch under the trees to an arable field.

Use the left hand field edge path, which skirts the back garden fence of the cottage previously passed, and then becomes a 3 metre wide grassy strip between two fields.

The white woodwork of St Andrew's tower comes into view. The grassy strip upgrades to a headland track. Nestled on the far side of the valley, surrounded by trees and the buildings of the Hall and Hall Farm, the church is central to a charming scene.

The track chicanes left-right through a gate and over a concrete bridge to climb to Hall Farm. Through the white gate is the road access and parking for the church. The church naturally attracts visitors from far and near. It has serenity in its antiquity and it is unpretentious in its workaday role. It is easy to discern the appeal of the place.

The return to Chipping Ongar is shared with the Essex Way, a long distance footpath from Harwich to Epping. South of the church gate is the entrance to the Hall. Enter here to pass Church Lodge by the lime trees, and to find the white stile under a horse chestnut tree. Enter the grazing field here and leave the pond on the right hand side to cross mid-field to the eastern gate and stile. The path follows the left hand field edge parallel to the wider drive on the other side of the fence. Where the drive bends southward, a gate in the fence allows a crossing of the drive to be made. A stile opposite marks the entrance to a mid-field headland track. This track makes a straight continuation gently down to re-cross Cripsey Brook, where it reforms as Bransons Lane and connects with the car parking where the walk began.

Historical Notes

Public Clock: Budworth Hall with the clock tower by the car park was built in 1886 as a memorial to Capt. P Budworth, a local historian who lived at Greensted Hall.

The Castle: This motte and bailey castle was strategically built at the confluence of the Cripsey brook and Roding river. The

WALK 6

outer bailey to the west of the castle enclosed the medieval town.
It was visited by several kings of the period including Henry II.

St Andrew's Church: This is rightly famous as the only surviving
log church in England. Although the building predated its
becoming a church, it certainly was a church in 1013 when the St
Edmund's body was rested there briefly on its funeral procession
to Bury St Edmunds. Its nave is built of oak logs split vertically
in halves and set vertically into an oak sill.

Church of St Martin of Tours: The Norman church typifies the
importance of Chipping Ongar during the post Conquest period.

New House Farm was for a time farmed by three of the Tol-
puddle Martyrs after they were pardoned in 1836. Alas, they were
the objects of local emnity, despite their pardon, and all three
emigrated to Canada, where they ended their days.

40

Walton On The Naze – Salt, Sand and Smugglers

Introduction: The coast of Tendring District in north-east Essex attracts many holiday makers. It is advertised as the Sunshine Coast, and there is sound meteorological evidence to support the claim. Tendring's coast of glorious sandy beaches strand over several miles from St Osyth Point to Stone Point. Walton on the Naze is right in the heart of this scene. In winter anglers get the pier to themselves. Dinghy sailors know of Walton Backwaters all the year round. Walton has two seasides back to back, but very different. The beach is a coast of attrition, where waves nibble and devour the land. Look at The Naze cliffs tumbling away all too readily. Behind them the tidal creeks of Hamford Water demonstrate the more usual type of Essex coast, of saltmarshes and mudflats: a coast ideal for the smuggling which was rife here in the 18th century.

Distance: A walking distance of 8 kilometres takes 2 hours to stroll. The ordnance survey sheet TM 22 covers the route at the pathfinders' scale of 1:25 000. The ramble is described anti-clockwise from the railway station at Walton on the Naze, map referenced TM 251214.

Refreshments: At a guess, every third establishment in Walton's tourist thoroughfares are eating or drinking or licking places of one sort or another. In winter there are still a good proportion of pubs for the size of the town, and a few kiosks serve the sea anglers.

How to get there: By road; from Colchester, follow the coastal traffic signs for Frinton, Walton & Clacton onto the A133. At

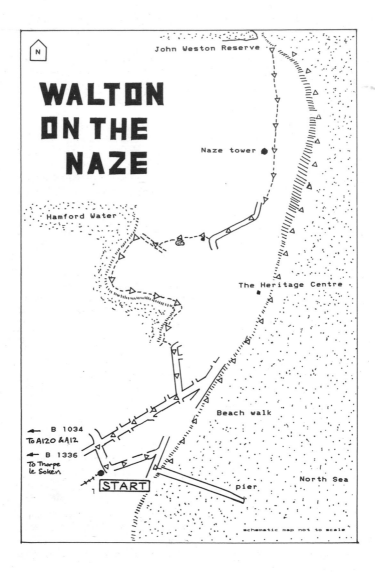

Weeley roundabout fork left for the B1034, B1033 and B1336 roads leading to Walton church. The station is signposted just uphill from the church crossroads. Park in the station car park. By Rail; London Liverpool Street to Walton on the Naze, change at Thorpe le Soken. By Bus; regular services from Colchester and from Clacton on Sea arrive at Kino Road bus depot.

The walk: From the station, smell the ozone and head for the pier. Descend by the Royal National Lifeboat Station with its clock, to use slope or steps to get to the base of Pier Hotel by the pier. Go left on The Parade and literally head northwards towards Felixstowe until there is no more land to walk upon. Some tides allow a beach walk, and the map shows this option. But usually it is the cliff route described here which is followed. The broad greensward on the Naze allows an alternative return route. The Kings Hotel marks the beginning of The Esplanade by the Kino Road bus station. East Terrace comes next and is followed as far as HM Coastguard Rescue Centre. Behind it is the old lifeboat station now housing The Heritage Centre.

Continue on the greensward to Green Lane, which like East Terrace has a dead end. Cross a second grassed zone to join the road by a footpath sign opposite 'Poplars'. Follow the footpath to a higher track joined by a green tiled house sporting a swimming pool in its front garden.

Join the track climbing towards the Naze Tower. This is a Trinity House seamark. Nearby are warnings of unstable cliffs.

The Naze open space extends beyond the octagonal tower, and the little stone inscribed with verse 3 of Psalm 63, to merge via nature trails with the nearby nature reserve. Dip with the slope as the cliffs diminish and find the wall between the upper beach scape ponds and the John Weston Nature Reserve.

The land from here to Stone Point is unprotected by seawalls and its saltings are likely to be covered at exceptionally high tides. This is the point to turn left and remain with the seawall. This too, is the extent of the right of way.

Ahead is a good view of the old naval port of Harwich with its modern commercial extension across the Orwell at Felixstowe. North Sea ferries disappear and re-appear to and from Parkeston on the Stour behind Harwich. The left horizon comprises the

Oakley-Beaumont ridge enclosing Hamford Water and its low islands.

An about turn here is advised. The Naze is a glorious open space with many paths, so a different route can be used to get back to the Naze Tower. From there go back along the track to the road by the home named 'Poplars', noticed earlier.

Continue downhill on the pavement as far as the sharp bend by the fish and chip shop. On the outside of the bend a footpath goes by house number 127. Follow the path by the pond under the willow tree and along by the dyke to Foundry Lane. Turn right along the lane, widened now the creek has been infilled, to find the old concrete barges at Foundry Quay. Go left over the stile to gain the seawall path which follows the left fork in the deeper channels. Pass the Anglian Water Authority enclosure to get close to some permanent housing.

Leave by house number 71 and cross Stratford Place to use any of Saville, Standley, North or Parsonage streets to get the main street of Walton. Turn inland by the Co-op stores and walk through to the Church. Turn left uphill to the Station, where the walk began.

Historical Notes

Smuggling: This stretch of coast with its sands and low cliffs was ideal for smuggling. The large Revenue cutters were unable to pursue small craft through the shallow offshore waters and so the smugglers were able to reach the safety of the secluded backwaters. During its heyday in the 18th century, whole communities were involved in this industry. Smuggled goods included lace, silks, coffee, gold and playing cards.

Pier: The Victorian pier is over 600 metres long. Paddle steamers no longer call there but it is still popular with sea-anglers, and with children of all ages!

Martello Tower: The martello tower is one of a chain along the coast dating from the Napoleonic wars.

Naze Tower: The Naze Tower dates from 1894. It is a Trinity House seamark – and very helpful too for the smugglers who plied this coast.

Prehistory: Neolothic remains from 200 metres below the sea are washed ashore occasionally. Coastal erosion, has meant that many earlier settlements have vanished beneath the waves.

Backwaters: Hamford Water is a Site of Special Scientific Interest. Horsey Island is inhabited. It is reached via The Wade from Kirby le Soken at low tides and then with four-wheel drive vehicles. Otherwise, boats or light aircraft are used. On Skippers island, a rota of wardens protect the wildlife there during appropriate nesting seasons.

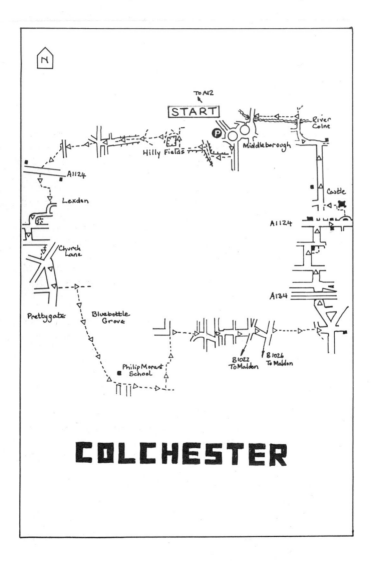

N

To A12

START

River Colne

Middleborough

Hilly Fields

A1124

Lexden

Castle

A1124

Church Lane

A134

Prettygate

Bluebottle Grove

B1022 To Maldon

B1026 To Maldon

Philip Morant School

COLCHESTER

Roman Colchester

Introduction: Colchester rates with Kings Lynn, Cambridge, Norwich and Bury St Edmunds as an attractive place to visit in East Anglia. This Essex town was once the seat of kings. The town centre has a Roman grid street layout situated on a hilltop above a defensive curve of the river Colne. Its fortifications are completed in the south by the Roman river – tributary of the Colne – and in the west by a series of Iron Age earthworks.

The town still hosts heavy industry and enjoys the advantages of a large military garrison and the University of Essex within close proximity, and Hythe port lies near the tidal limit of the Colne. This Ramble is routed to sample several epochs of Colchester (the Roman Camulodunum) and to give good views over the Colne valley countryside.

Distance: The walking distance is 8 kilometres which takes about 2 hours to stroll. Ordnance Survey sheet TL 92 covers the route at the pathfinders' scale of 1:25 000. The ramble is described anti-clockwise, starting from the car park beside the A134 approach to the town at Sheepen Place, map referenced TL 992255.

Refreshments: The Marquis of Granby at the foot of North Hill, and The Victoria in North Station Road are two pubs near to the start of the Ramble. About halfway around, Lexden Road is crossed close to The Crown, just up the hill, and to The Sun, just down the hill by St Leonard's Church. Otherwise there are many pubs and cafes towards the end of the Ramble in Colchester's town centre.

How to get there: Use the A12 entry into Colchester from the A604 roundabout at Stanway signposted with an elephant emblem as an exit for Colchester Zoo. From London direction, pass under the roundabout and take the next slip road left. From Ipswich and the east, use the roundabout to U turn and head back eastwards on the A12, only to take the next slip road left. The slip road is signed '(A134)'. It steers traffic under the dual carriageway to a roundabout. Take the second exit from the roundabout to go eastwards along Remembrance Avenue to Colnebank roundabout. Take the third exit this time to use the dual carriageway of the A134 to the foot of Balkerne Hill. There is a multi-storey car park by the junction of Sheepen Place with Middleborough; and an open car park in Sheepen Road opposite.

The Walk: Starting from the Middleborough roundabout, use the pedestrian crossings and underpass to get to the western pavement of Balkerne Hill. Face the oncoming traffic down the dual carriageway as far as the end of the road by the Water Board installations. Turn right away from the old Roman Wall, onto a path waymarked 'To Lexden'. The path contours the hill beneath St Mary's hospital to a stiled entry to a small paddock. The exit stile is in the next lower corner. Enter a double hedged path and after a few paces, climb some rough steps up a gravel slope to the left.

Now on Hilly Fields, one of the precious few open spaces in Colchester, keep to the main path which follows the left hand hedge up as far as the sports field fence. Turn right to have this fence on the left hand side and follow it around until the westward direction is resumed. This path offers good vantage viewing over Remembrance Avenue, the river Colne, the railway activity and to the countryside of West Bergholt and Braiswick on the further side of the Colne valley.

Leave the north west fence corner of the sports area to use a main path contouring the open space. It converges with others at an exit stile from Hilly Fields by an old pill box.

Fences steer the path, still contouring the valley side, to the housing estate by Lexden Grange. The path continues as Elianore Road and crosses Glen Avenue to the entrance to Bramley Close. Sharing the junction is a footpath diverging left of the Close. Also of interest is the rare royal mail box by the crossing.

Gardens steer the path over Hurnard Drive and down to the paddock overlooking Colchester Camping ground. Footfalls have scored the grass to the exit stile and short path to Spring Lane. Turn right down the lane to bridge left over the spring and enter the open space known as Lexden Springs. The grass spreads upwards to some trees on Lexden Hill. A hedge forms the southern boundary. A speed restriction sign just visible above the hedge, marks the target to find the exit gap.

Cross the road to a footpath barricade and climb the tarmac path to go right on Marlowe Way of the poets' estate. Go right again to find Lexden mount under the cedar trees.

From the ancient tumuli, go across Wordsworth Road to enter Masefield Drive and turn left onto Thompson Avenue. Beside dwelling number 36 a footpath links to Shakespeare Road. Go left at the bottom and cross Church Lane with care to enter Parsons Hill.

At the top turn left, by Magazine Farmhouse, to use a bridleway crossing Lexden Park to Bluebottle Grove. The Grove is signposted as an ancient monument, and it is possible to walk along it providing the debris of the October 1987 hurricane has been cleared away. From its southern end, a gravel path continues around the fence of the Philip Morant School and across to some allotment gardens on the right hand side. Turn left here to stay between gardens and school playing fields until there are yet more school fields on the right hand side.

At the corner of Park Road follow the school field boundary right to enter an urban path which leads through to Queens Road. At the road's further end chicane left-right across Cambridge Road to enter Creffield Road by the rear entrances to Colchester's Royal Grammar School. Continue over Maldon Road and climb Beaconsfield Road to Butt Road. A few metres to the left a green water tower may be seen. Cross towards this to find the entry steps of Artillery Folly. The folly continues off its eastern end as Walsingham Road which joins Napier Road at the top of St John's Green.

Along the top side of the Green is the Abbey Gateway commanding a good view northwards over Colchester's roofscape. In the lowest corner by the school is the pass under the Southway dual carriageway. Use this and cross the next road to enter the town centre by the shop-lined passage rising to Scheregate steps. The elegant town hall clock tower is in view above Trinity Street. Approach the town hall via Holy Trinity church now housing a museum, and Pelham's Lane. Turn right to use the High Street as far as the war memorial opposite the Tourist Information Office.

Enter the castle park by the memorial and explore at will. The castle contains a museum, as do both Hollytrees House alongside it, and All Saints Church opposite. Ornamental and restful gardens surround the Keep, and at the river level, beyond further remnants of the Roman town wall, are various sports facilities.

From near the northwest corner of the castle a minor tarmac path peels off the main paths to a pedestrians' gate on to Ryedale Road. Use this gate and cross the road to pass beneath the upper storey of a house and find St Helen's Chapel. Go down Maidenburgh Street, by the excavated theatre, to Northgate Street. Turn right around the castle park's Rye Gate railings to find Middleborough Mill bridge leading on to Kings Meadow. Follow the riverbank path upstream to North Station Road bridge in the vicinity of the starting place.

Historical Notes

Roman Colchester: The Roman City of Camulodunum occupied a site of 108 acres. Balkerne Hill is bounded by part of the walls. Balkerne Gate was the main gate of Roman Colchester and is celebrated as the most impressive Town Gate in Roman Britain. Now re-opened to pedestrians, it makes a grand entrance to the Mercury Theatre.

Colchester Castle: The castle had the largest keep ever built in Europe. When it was built in the late 11th century it measured 151 by 110 feet, considerably larger than the White Tower in London. The upper stages were removed in 1683, and the present top structures of the keep belong to the mid 18th century. The castle now houses one of the best collections of Romano-British finds on view to the public. Within the castle museum is a model of the Temple of Claudius. This is a conjectural reconstruction of the building which once stood on the castle site. The substructure of the original temple can be seen in the massive vaults under the Norman Keep.

An obelisk behind the castle marks the execution spot for the

Royalist commanders Lucas and Lisle defeated by Fairfax in the Siege of Colchester in 1648.

The castle park was presented to the town by Viscount Cowdray, a member of Parliament for Colchester sometimes known as the 'Member for Mexico'. His engineering ventures included founding oil recovery companies in Mexico, which still echo in the syllable 'mex' found in the name of many petrol filling stations.

St John's Abbey was founded by Eudo Dapifer in 1096 of the Benedictine Order. Only the gatehouse, as seen from the Green, remains today despite damage suffered in the Siege of Colchester 1648.

Trinity Street has house plaques denoting John Wilbye and William Gilberd. Gilberd was a physician and scientist who won fame for first realising the essential connection between electricity and magnetism.

Middle Mill was the penultimate waterwheel on the river Colne. The next Mill at Easy Bay marks the tidal limit of the Colne.

Middleborough was the site for the livestock market between the time when it was sited in High Street and the present site in Severalls Lane. Originally it could have been an open marshalling place for traffic waiting to enter the walled town.

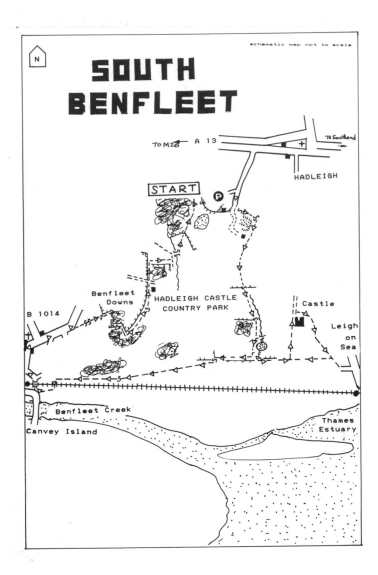

Hadleigh Castle Country Park

Introduction: The establishment of a country park by the Thames Estuary at Hadleigh received planning permission in 1974. It took a great deal of voluntary effort from the Hadleigh Castle Country Park Conservation Group, set up in 1980, to help bring about the opening of the Park in 1987. The result is a truly magnificent open air lung, largely hidden from the landward side by the dense urban settlements of Thameside. But from the deck of a ferry using Sheerness port across the Thames, the sylvan scene is glorious on its rising ground. Yet it is the walker in the Park who really savours the solace it can provide.

The spurs and re-entrants of Benfleet Downs give the landscape a truly Down-like appearance. The saltmarshes within the southern seawall carry a busy commuter railway service between Leigh on Sea (for Shoeburyness) and Benfleet (for London, Fenchurch Street).

Indeed this ramble extends from 8 to 14 kilometres if a ride is not taken on the railway.

The sentry duty of Hadleigh Castle was as a defence against seaborn invaders. In reality it has defended the hinterland from housing development. Many people will unite to resist any attempts to destroy the castle; and when they defend the castle they protect the environs too. The Castle is a catalyst for the open space around it. Much of the land around the castle is farmed by the Salvation Army, and its Colony Farm too, keeps the land's use intact.

Below the cliffs, cockles are landed at Leigh on Sea, Brent geese and other waders feed off the mudflats around Two Tree Island. Oil and gas products tranship on Canvey Island. Sea vessels of many sizes slide by in channels selected to suit their depths so binoculars are handy here.

Distance: A walking distance of 8 kilometres takes about 2 hours. To this must be added about 10 minutes for the train journey. There is not likely to be much waiting; trains are as frequent as two per hour even on a winter Sunday. Without the ride, the walk extends to 14 kilometres and takes 3½ hours plus picnic or stopping time. Ordnance Survey sheets TQ 78 and TQ 88 cover the route at the pathfinders' scale of 1:25 000. The ramble is described clockwise from the Chapel Lane car park in Hadleigh Castle Country Park, map referenced TQ 801869.

Refreshments: Leigh on Sea. Several inns are to be found along the Front. Likewise there are more inns at South Benfleet, notably the three pubs by the church. At Hadleigh, there are two pubs by the island where the church and fire station separate the carriageways of the A13 road.

How to get there: By the A130 road Chelmsford–Canvey Island Road, which intersects the A127 road (M25 link) at Rayleigh. Turn east on to the A13 (another M25 link) road at Benfleet and climb Thundersley's Bread and Cheese Hill to Hadleigh. Where the carriageways divide in Hadleigh, perform a legitimate U-turn by the church. Proceed westwards to the memorial by the recreation ground. Turn left by the chapel to enter Chapel Lane car park, complete with conveniences, off the further end of the Lane. By train; to either Leigh on Sea or to South Benfleet. Both are on the Shoeburyness–Fenchurch Street line. By bus; to Hadleigh, Leigh on Sea Station, or South Benfleet Station. The area is well served by a mixture of bus services at frequent intervals.

The walk: From the Country Park car park, go back to Chapel Lane, turn right to the farm gate. A sign declares footpath No 2. Perhaps the 8 has been erased, as it is actually number 28. Enter the yard and swing left on the main track to the anglers' car park and reservoir bank. A further waymark, points left of the embankment. Proceed to the gate at the north east corner where a third waymark points to sea. Pass the eastern embankment and enter the grazing land by passing a flat topped workshop and steering for the stile in the fence lower down the re-entrant.

Across further grassland, 100 metres after the stile, a fourth waymark directs the path slighty left to a row of trees marking a stream springing from beneath the sands of Sandpit Hill. Waymarks are nailed to the largest oak and ash trees in the row. Another stile is crossed and the path comes alongside a cart-bridge over the enlarging stream on the left hand side. A swampy pond blocks the way ahead. Go right onto the track off the bridge and follow the marks on the grass around to a fence where a triple signpost marks the junction of path 28 with path 12. This spot will be visited again later if the train option is not used.

Go left on path 12 to the field corner. Cross the stile and use the field edge path parallel to the railway. Another triple sign-post indicates that the cart track leading up to Hadleigh Castle is right of way number 27. From near the castle entrance path 11 takes a high level route along the northside of the ruins' bound-ary. It is easily followed down the ridge to merge with path 12 at the foot of the slope. Continue along path 12 which is a field edge path with ditch on the left hand side.

The path becomes renumbered 86 and edges another field to the stile at the western end of Castle Drive. Continue through to Belton Way West and turn downhill to the railway station for a train to Benfleet.

To ride or not to ride. That is the question usually answered by the weather. Sometimes it is a good time to let the train shield you from the rain. If it is fine and your feet are comfortable you may prefer to continue rambling. If so then back-track up Belton Way and along Castle drive and around the field edges to the junction of path 11 with path 12. Stay low this time and keep to path 12, contouring to the stile beyond the foot of the castle ruins.

Go by the junction with path 28 and follow the fence parallel to the railway line, one field away. At the next stile, the path reverts to the southern side of the fence, and stays there, wet or dry, gradually converging with the railway line. Beyond the western tip of the country park a stile by a metal gate is found adjacent to the line. The path continues as a causeway to a white railway gate. Here the line is crossed. It is necessary to be decisive about the action to be taken. If the lines are clear, cross quickly. There is no build up between the rails, so a high knee lift is needed. The curve of the track impedes some visibility. On the southern side is the B1014 road bending to cross Benfleet Creek over to Canvey Island.

To the right is the station where those who took the train rejoin the walk. Opposite is the pleasant Queens View garden by the bus stops. The railway station entrance has a tunnel nearby. Use this to get to the landward side of the track and enter High Street. Follow High Street around to the Church of St Mary the Virgin, ignore High Road to continue up the hill of the B1014 still. There is some height to be gained, and the pavement has a gentle incline and a noisy background. Go beyond the speed limit increase sign by Norwood Drive and fork right on to a path beginning by a gas sub-station. It starts as a field edge path, and then a pair of stiles in tandem take it to a narrow section between fence and ditch.

Another stile gives entry to a Y-shaped grazing plot, both arms of which offer uphill walking. Take the left hand one which carries the right of way towards a drinking trough at its upper end. As the trough is approached, a waymarked stile comes into view on the right hand side. Cross this to use the left hand field edge path.

In the corner next to the trees a waymark indicates that the path follows the edge of the same field around the corner and still climbing. The next waymark is at a grand vantage point overlooking Canvey Island and the Thames shipping lanes with Kent in the distance. Turn left to enter a fenced path under the canopy of trees. The fences steer the path around a right angled bend and then to a waymarked left turn.

Now in the park at last, path 13 loses its right hand fence. Occasionally good views across the Downs to Hadleigh Castle are available through breaks in the shrubbery. Follow the strong line of the grazing fence contouring on the left hand side. A stile carries the path outside the park, still against the grazing fence, but now with a garden orchard fence on the right hand side too. At the far end the cottage drive is crossed to find a stiled re-entrance to the park.

A walk down a delightful glade ensues. It finishes at a bridge and stile. Go right alongside the stream just crossed to the confluence with Kersey Brook. Go left a few paces to the culvert bridge where a waymark reads 'CARPARK' and points north-eastwards. This is path 29, diagonally crossing the hillside grazing to the wooded corner. Under the trees the path is fenced and eventually the junction right for Chapel Lane car park becomes clearly visible.

Historical Notes

Farm Colony: 1000 acres of farmland near to Chapel Lane car park were purchased in 1891 by General Booth for The Salvation Army.

Stanley T. Jermyn, naturalist and author of *Flora of Essex* was born in 1909 in this part of south Essex.

Hadleigh Castle was originally a late Norman construction by Hubert de Burgh but was rebuilt by Edward III in the late 13th century. Building materials, valuable in Essex, have been taken from the site over the years. Now it is protected. However, the ravages of coastal erosion cannot be totally halted and parts of the outer castle have slipped away with the land. The Tate gallery has a painting of the castle by Constable.

Railway: Down below the castle's site, the railway dates from 1855.

Cockles: Leigh on Sea's shingle beach houses a cockle industry. Fishermen labour their catch ashore in baskets straining from their yoked shoulders as they bounce on crude plank gangways.

Nature Reserve: Two Tree Island is a nature reserve of great variety. Its habitat offers eel grass as great attraction for Brent geese. On other parts of the mudflats, dunlin (also called stints) dart around the tide line like feathered fieldmice.

Canvey Island: Sir Henry Appleton hired Dutch drainage expertise in 1622 to embank the island. The work of Vermuyden and Croppenburgh has stood the test of time. A Dutch style cottage remains on the island as a memorial link.

Canvey is sometimes a butt for cruel jokes. Its riverside industrial activities are not only integral to the prosperity of the country, they have attracted housing too. The people apply pressure for safeguards against the inherent dangers. The bridge was improved in 1924 and the new A130 bridge followed half a century later to improve the link to mainland Essex.

Benfleet Creek: Bridgebuilders for roads and rail have uncovered relics from the Battle of Benfleet in 894 AD.

Smuggling: In the 18th century this part of the Thames Estuary was a haven for smugglers. Small trading schooners could hide among the oyster dredgers and make well organised transfers of contraband.

Braintree

Introduction: Braintree is a fine town with good views over its verdant valleys. Situated in Mid-Essex on a narrow ridge between the valley of the river Blackwater and the valley of its major tributary the river Brain, it is rewarding to explore. Modern shopping facilities, the creation of a new walk to Dunmow and the celebration of the scholar John Ray's work encourages many visitors.

Distance: A walking distance of 7 kilometres takes about 2 hours to stroll.

The Ordnance Survey sheet TL 72 covers the route at the pathfinders' scale of 1:25 000. The ramble is here described clockwise starting from Station Approach in Braintree, map referenced TL 760227.

Refreshments: The Spread Eagle in Coldnailhurst Avenue is just a few paces off the route. Other pubs, cafes and restaurants are situated not too far from the Heritage Centre by Market Square.

How to get there: By road; from junction 8 of the M11 motorway head along the A120 road east of Stansted Airport and Great Dunmow. A one way system operates clockwise in Braintree. Stay with the A120 through to the traffic lights 400 metres beyond the White Hart. Turn right here to join westbound traffic. Ignore all junctions left or right until by the railway station in Station Approach, where there is a car park. By Train; Braintree is the terminus of a branch line from the mainline at Witham. By bus; the bus station is in Victoria Street, about 3 minutes walk north of the railway station. Services link with Chelmsford, Colchester and Bishops Stortford, plus local village services.

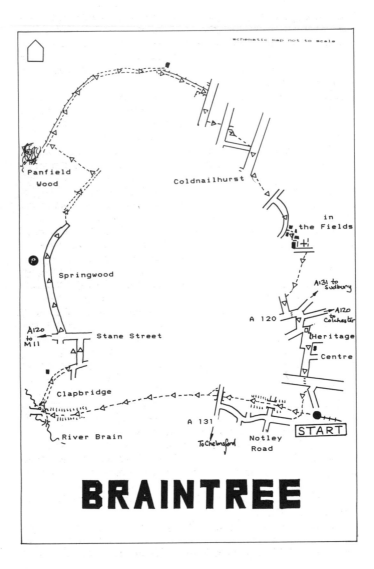

schematic map not to scale

Panfield Wood

Coldnailhurst

in the Fields

A131 to Sudbury

Springwood

A120 to Colchester

A 120

Heritage Centre

A120 to M11

Stane Street

Clapbridge

A 131

River Brain

To Chelmsford

Notley Road

START

BRAINTREE

The walk: Part of the railway track no longer carrying rails is used as a car park. Join the track between house number 40 Station Approach and the Swimming Pool. Head westwards towards Dunmow. It is a very pleasant walk created by the Community Programme. The bridge over Notley Road was exciting to cross.

Next time, if the bridge is not more substantial by then, a diversion will be selected. It will use St Johns Avenue from the Swimming Pool across to Godlings Way and so to join the track down a purpose built ramp from the A131 road.

It is easy to stroll along the old railway track, gathering steam enough to get to Rayne without realising the turn off has been missed. There are two safeguards against this mistake. One, use a watch to time 15 minutes from the A131 road bridge. Two, be observant and look out for the meanders of the river Brain in the fields below, and stay Braintree side of the river.

The turn off takes the form of a farm-gated level crossing. Each gate has a stile and beyond them, to the left below, a footbridge over the river. Uphill to the right is the foursquare farmhouse of Claphridge Farm. Share the wide gravel drive up by the farm to find the exit onto Clare Road. Use the first left turn on to Francis Road and the next left onto Rayne Road.

Opposite is Springwood Drive. It has good pavement passing the factory entrances and side drives named Elliott, Bradbury, Swinborne, Warner, Crittall, etc. From the car park to Springwood's far terminus a footpath is parallel with the Drive. This path continues through the gap in the north-west hedge corner and follows a change crop alignment under wires carried on wooden poles.

Now in the countryside with Panfield Wood one field away on the left hand side, the white painted sails of Bocking Post Mill come into view on the far side of the Pant valley.

Where the overhead wires turn right, make the opposite turn to the left before crossing the culvert. A further change crop alignment leads the path towards a line of poplar trees, planted as if to form a handrail to Panfield Wood. Turn right on the grassy headland and pass beside the row of trees leading towards Park Farm.

As the farm track enters the farmyard, so the footpath takes to the right hand side of the hedge end on the right hand side of the track. The field edge path follows this hedge to make an exit

61

between garden fences. Now on Panfield Lane by a layby outside house number 294, turn right to the next lay-by at number 270. Go left here to find the greenery of an urban open space sweeping down the valley side. Tack across this space from Currants Farm Road diagonally right to the junction of Meadow Side with Coadnailhurst Avenue. Go right to Arnhem Way to find a continuation of the greensward still spreading down the hillside. Several tarmac paths radiate from the footbridge at the bottom. Use one of these to cross the bridge and to begin the climb up the ridge to Braintree's town centre.

The path from the footbridge leads to a road junction. Continue straight ahead into the crescent of Rosemary Avenue as far as the change in house numbering from 70 to 46. In the gap a footpath passes an electricity sub-station to serpentine between garden fences and to emerge in Hills Close by St Peter Bocking Church. Go around to the far corner of the church where St Peter's Close crosses St Peter's in the Field and St Peter's Walk. Nearby is a very pleasant public garden.

Use the Walk behind Causeway House, the headquarters of Braintree District Council to join Panfield Lane again. Turn left to Rayne Road and use the pedestrian crossing over the Roman Stane Street to get to the statue of John Ray looking down Coggeshall Road beside The White Hart.

Cross Bank Street to get to the Swan on Little Square. Three passages allow progress through to Market Square. Each one is captivating and unique to Braintree. Why not lace a way using all three? It is worth exploring. South from the Swan, around to the fire station and tower of Drury Lane. Back to the Swan and thread down Leather Lane to the Wednesday market throng. Around to the left, across Manor Road from the Nags Head, is the Heritage Centre containing much information and periodic exhibitions. Below is the Post Office, cinema and Police Station. Pass all of these to get to the pedestrian crossing over to the Railway Tavern and an entrance to Station Approach, where the walk began.

Historical Notes

Braintree: Braintree is on a gravel capped ridge of clay. There is evidence of pre Roman settlement here, particularly near Skitts

Hill as overviewed from the Station at the beginning of this ramble. Stane Street, the Roman Road from St Albans to Colchester passes over the ridge between Rayne and Bradwell.

The town suffered some damage during 1648 when Lisle and Lucas and other Royalists passed through en route for Colchester and the consequent siege and executions.

Braintree is linked to Braintree, Massachusetts by its industrial vigour. Predominantly the industries are metal windows and, until recent times, man-made fibres such as Tricel and Dicel. Scientific and technological firms replace mills such as the razed factory at Bocking.

Old Railway Walk: The Braintree-Dunmow Walk is a public open space utilising the old railway trail extending from the Witham branch line to the Cambridge line at Bishops Stortford.

Indoor Arena: Towerland's roof silhouette looms large from near Park farm. It is an indoor arena in great demand, particularly for equestrianism and for bowling.

Windmill: Further away is the picturesque form of Bocking windmill dating from 1720 and recently restored by Friends of Bocking Windmill.

Nature Reserve: St Peters in the Fields nature reserve is located just a few paces downhill from the church. This must be the most urban location within the long list of Essex Naturalist Trust Reserves.

John Ray the English naturalist was born in nearby Black Notley in 1627, the son of a blacksmith. In 1649 he became a fellow of Trinity College Cambridge. He travelled extensively studying botany and zoology. Ray's classification of plants was the foundation of the 'Natural System' and formed the basis of all modern zoology.